C IS FOR CONSTITUTION

US Government Book for Kids
Children's Government Books

BABY PROFESSOR
EDUCATION KIDS

Speedy Publishing LLC
40 E. Main St. #1156
Newark, DE 19711
www.speedypublishing.com
Copyright 2017

All Rights reserved. No part of this book may be reproduced or used in any way or form or by any means whether electronic or mechanical, this means that you cannot record or photocopy any material ideas or tips that are provided in this book.

The United States is governed by a Constitution that sets out the basic laws of the country and establishes how the government should operate. Where did that document come from? Let's see!

THE NEED FOR A CONSTITUTION

When the United States became independent from Great Britain after the Revolutionary War, it was a loose collection of thirteen colonies along the east coast of North America. The colonies were very different, and each was suspicious that the other colonies might be trying to get ahead of them in some way.

REVOLUTIONARY WAR

GREAT BRITAIN FLAG

The colonies first put together the Articles of Confederation, a document for a central government, in 1781. This was while the colonies were still at war, and most people were concentrating on fighting Great Britain.

The Articles of Confederation set up a very weak central government, one that could not even set and collect taxes to get the money to do what it had to do. There were no federal courts and not even a president! The Congress was supposed to decide national matters, but it couldn't make any one of the thirteen states do what was decided if that state did not want to.

GEORGE WASHINGTON PRESIDING AT THE CONVENTION OF 1787 TO REVISE THE ARTICLES OF CONFEDERATION

ALEXANDER HAMILTON

After the United States became independent in 1783, it became clear that the Articles of Confederation were too weak to support an effective central government. Alexander Hamilton of New York sent out a call in 1786 for a constitutional convention to create a new central document and a new way of governing.

Each state was invited to send delegates to Philadelphia in 1787. Twelve states sent delegates; Rhode Island was worried about the federal government having too much power, and refused to participate.

THE RHODE ISLAND STATE HOUSE

DEBATING AND DECIDING

Starting in May, 1787, the delegates met in the same Philadelphia building where the Declaration of Independence was proclaimed at the start of the American Revolution. There were fifty-five men present. George Washington, who was a national hero because of his work as a general in the Revolution, was the president of the convention.

INDEPENDENCE HALL IN PHILADELPHIA, PENNSYLVANIA, USA.

ARTICLES OF CONFEDERATION AND PERPETUAL UNION BETWEEN THE STATES OF

NEW-HAMPSHIRE, MASSACHUSETTS-BAY, RHODE-ISLAND and PROVIDENCE PLANTATIONS, CONNECTICUT, NEW-YORK, NEW-JERSEY, PENNSYLVANIA, DELAWARE, MARYLAND, VIRGINIA, NORTH-CAROLINA, SOUTH-CAROLINA and GEORGIA.

LANCASTER, (PENNSYLVANIA,) Printed:
BOSTON, Re-printed by JOHN GILL, Printer to the GENERAL ASSEMBLY.
M,DCC,LXXVII.

THE ARTICLES OF CONFEDERATION

Among the delegates were businessmen, farmers, lawyers, and bankers. Many of them had fought in the Revolution, and most of them had been leaders in their state governments. There were no women delegates, and all the delegates were white.

The plan had been for the delegates to make edits to the Articles of Confederation. However, they soon agreed it would be easier to start fresh and create a brand-new document.

People held very different views of what a central government should be able to do, and what the states should still be able to do. Delegates remembered that one of the reasons for the Revolution was that the British government had too much power without the colonies (now states) being able to make their opinions heard.

HOUSES OF PARLIAMENT IN LONDON

THE US HOUSE OF REPRESENTATIVES AT THE CAPITOL BUILDING IN WASHINGTON D.C.

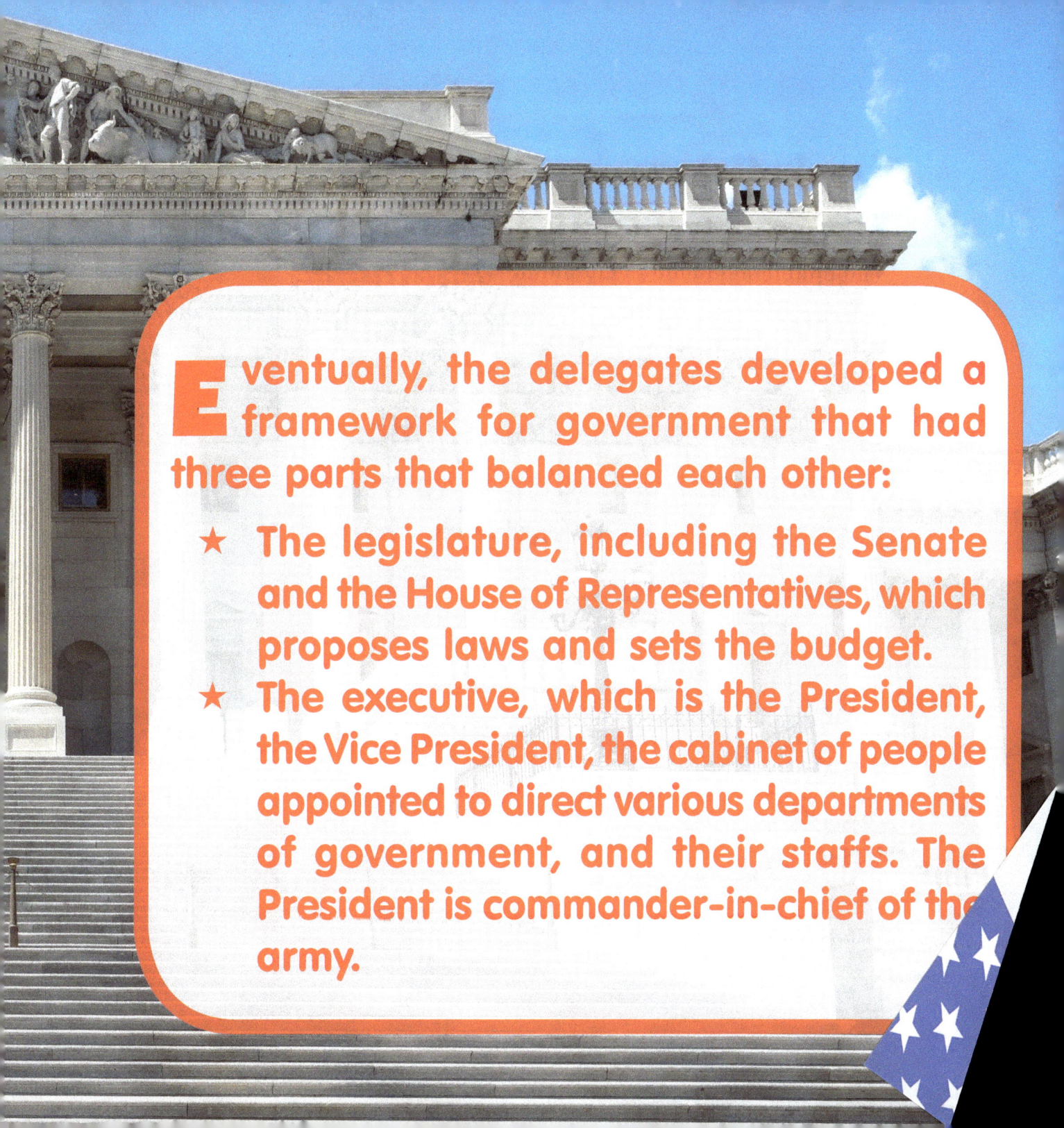

Eventually, the delegates developed a framework for government that had three parts that balanced each other:

★ The legislature, including the Senate and the House of Representatives, which proposes laws and sets the budget.

★ The executive, which is the President, the Vice President, the cabinet of people appointed to direct various departments of government, and their staffs. The President is commander-in-chief of the army.

★ **The judiciary, including the Supreme Court. The Supreme Court could decide whether a new law is "constitutional": that is, whether it fits in the framework of the Constitution. If the court decides a law is unconstitutional, nobody has to obey that law.**

The three branches of government work in a system of "checks and balances" so no one branch becomes too powerful.

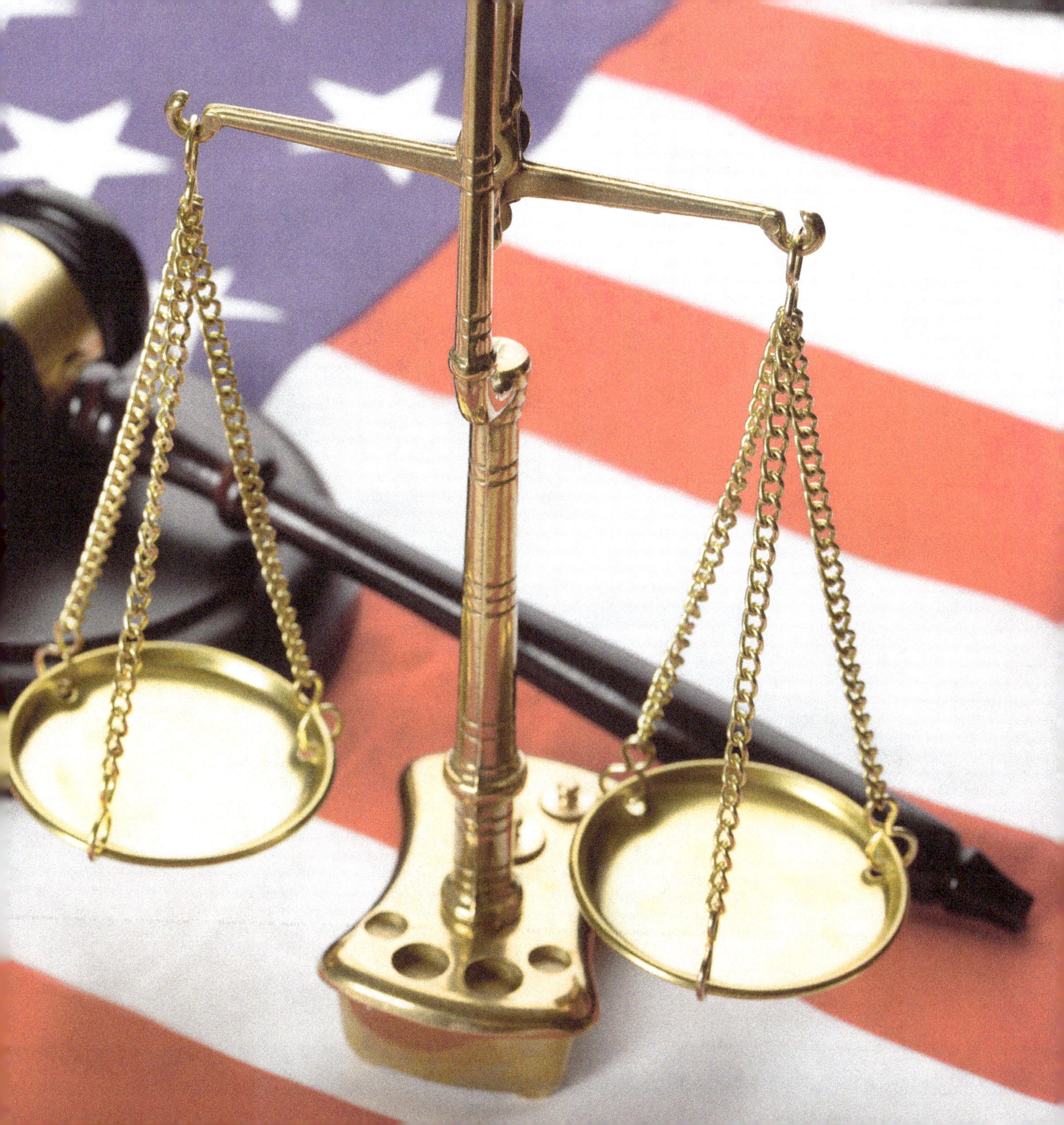

MEETING HALL

There are two houses, of equal power, in the legislature as a result of a compromise. The big states wanted the number of representatives to be based on population, while the small states wanted all states to have an equal voice. The compromise created the House of Representatives, where the number of representatives a state has depends on its population; and the Senate, where each state has two seats no matter how big or small it is.

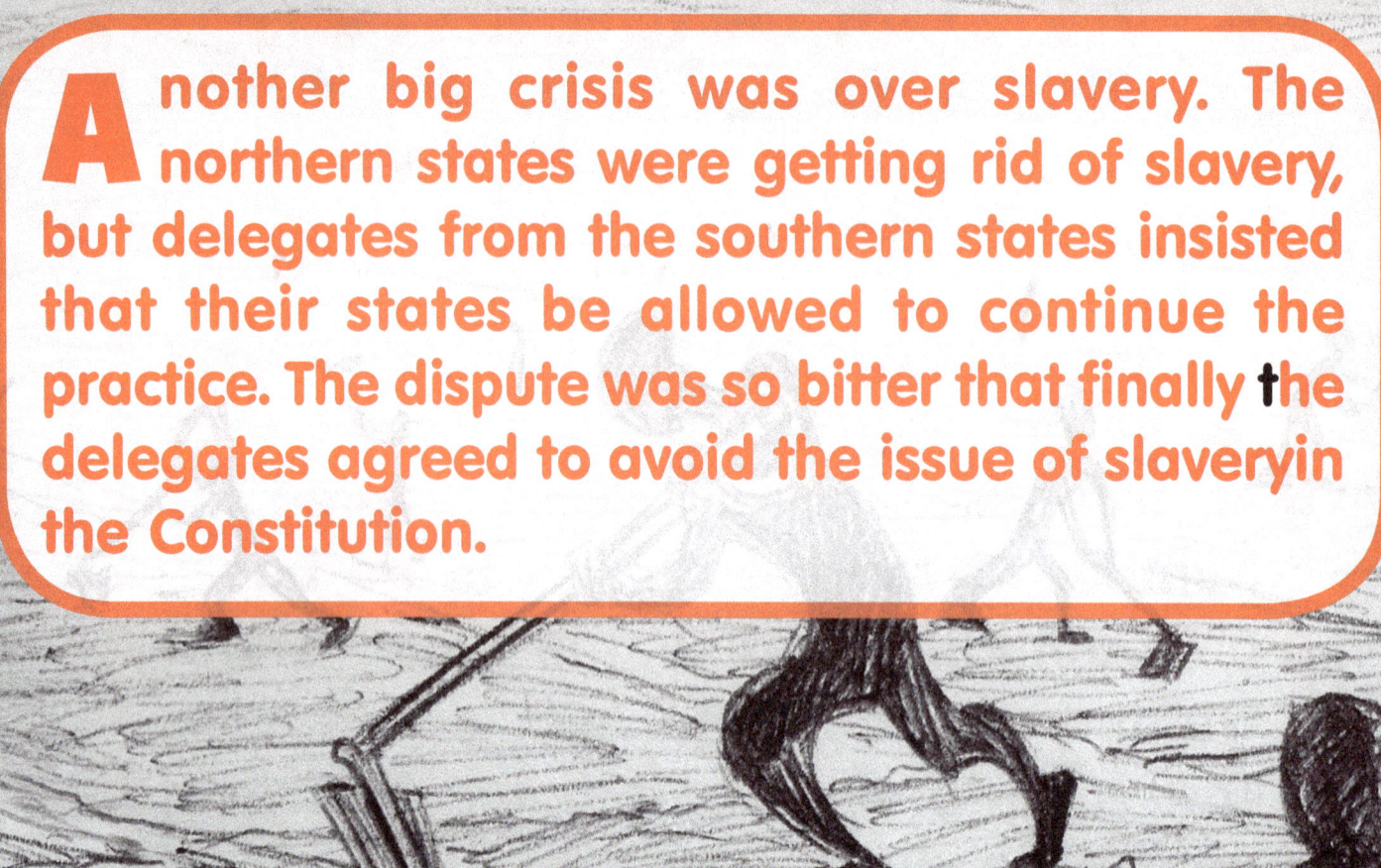

Another big crisis was over slavery. The northern states were getting rid of slavery, but delegates from the southern states insisted that their states be allowed to continue the practice. The dispute was so bitter that finally the delegates agreed to avoid the issue of slavery in the Constitution.

SLAVERY

TWO YOUNG ADULT WOMEN VOTING IN A VOTING BOOTH

For tax purposes, and for deciding the population of a state, the Constitution said a slave counts as three-fifths of a free person. (At this time women did not have the right to vote.) They also agreed that Congress could not even try to end the slave trade for thirty years, until 1808.

APPROVING THE CONSTITUTION

The final document was ready in September of 1787. George Washington was the first delegate to sign it. Some delegates refused to sign, and some had already gone home after a long summer of work.

To become law, the constitution had to be ratified ("agreed to") by two-thirds (nine) of the original thirteen states. By December of 1787, five states had ratified the Constitution.

SCENE AT THE SIGNING OF THE CONSTITUTION OF THE UNITED STATES

NEW HAMPSHIRE STATE HOUSE, CONCORD, NEW HAMPSHIRE, USA.

After that, progress became slower. Some states were afraid that the document gave too much power to the central government, and others resented that the scandal of slavery had not been resolved. Some delegates felt the document needed to include a statement of basic human rights.

Finally, in June, 1788, New Hampshire became the ninth state to ratify the Constitution. It became the law of the land as of March 4, 1789.

Rhode Island was the last of the states to ratify the Constitution. It did so in May of 1790.

THE RHODE ISLAND STATE HOUSE, THE CAPITOL OF THE U.S. STATE OF RHODE ISLAND.

UNITED STATES DECLARATION OF INDEPENDENCE

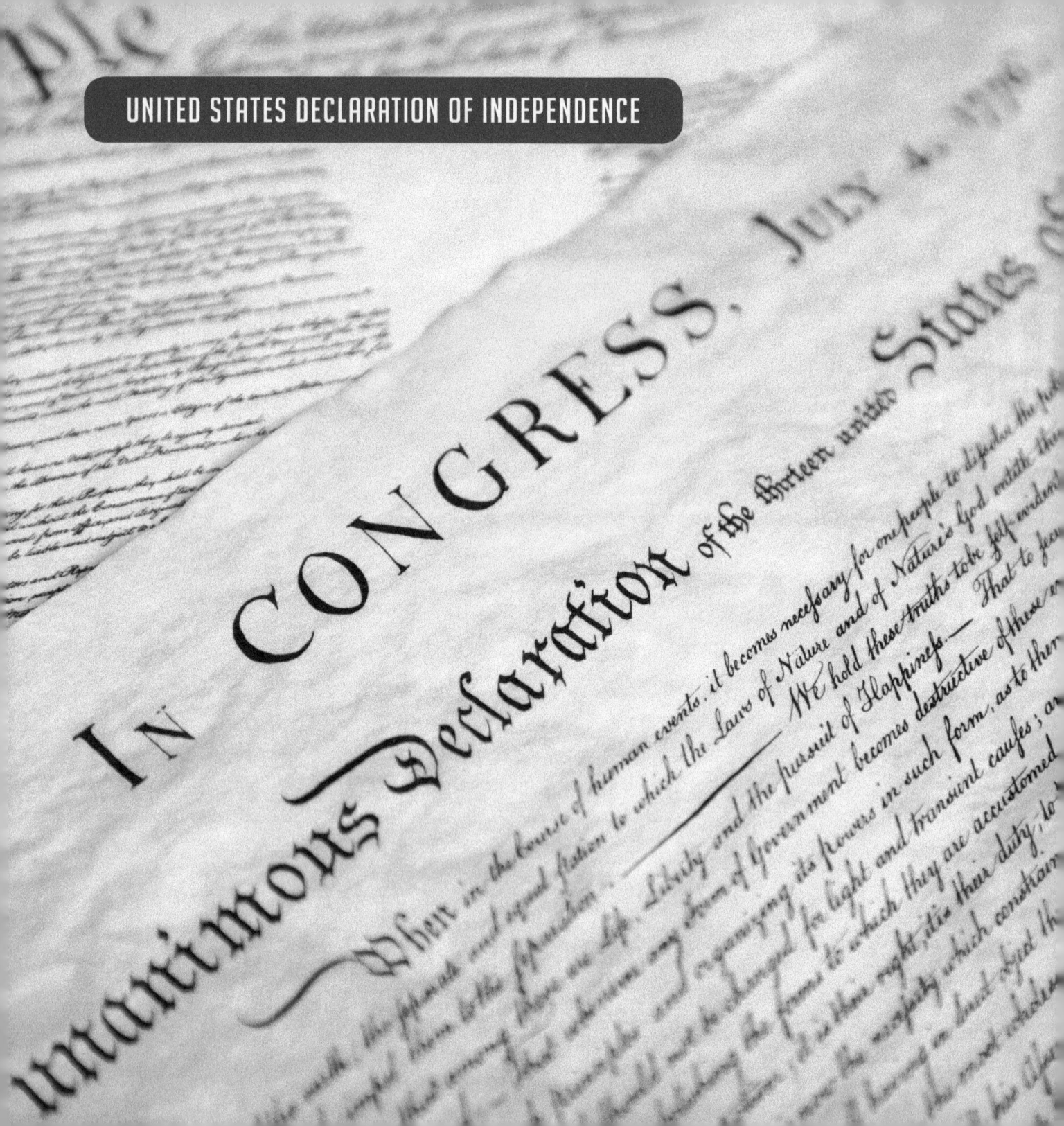

A LIVING DOCUMENT

The delegates knew they had not created a perfect system of government, so they put in place ways for the Constitution to be amended as the need for changing it became obvious. The process is difficult—it requires Congress to approve the amendment, the President to approve it, and for two-thirds of the states to ratify it before an amendment comes into effect.

Right away the government started working on a Bill of Rights, laying out basic rights like freedom of speech and freedom of religion that the government could not take away from people. Ten amendments make up the Bill of Rights, and they became part of the Constitution in 1791. Read about them in the Baby Professor book Does the Bill of Rights Give Me Freedom?

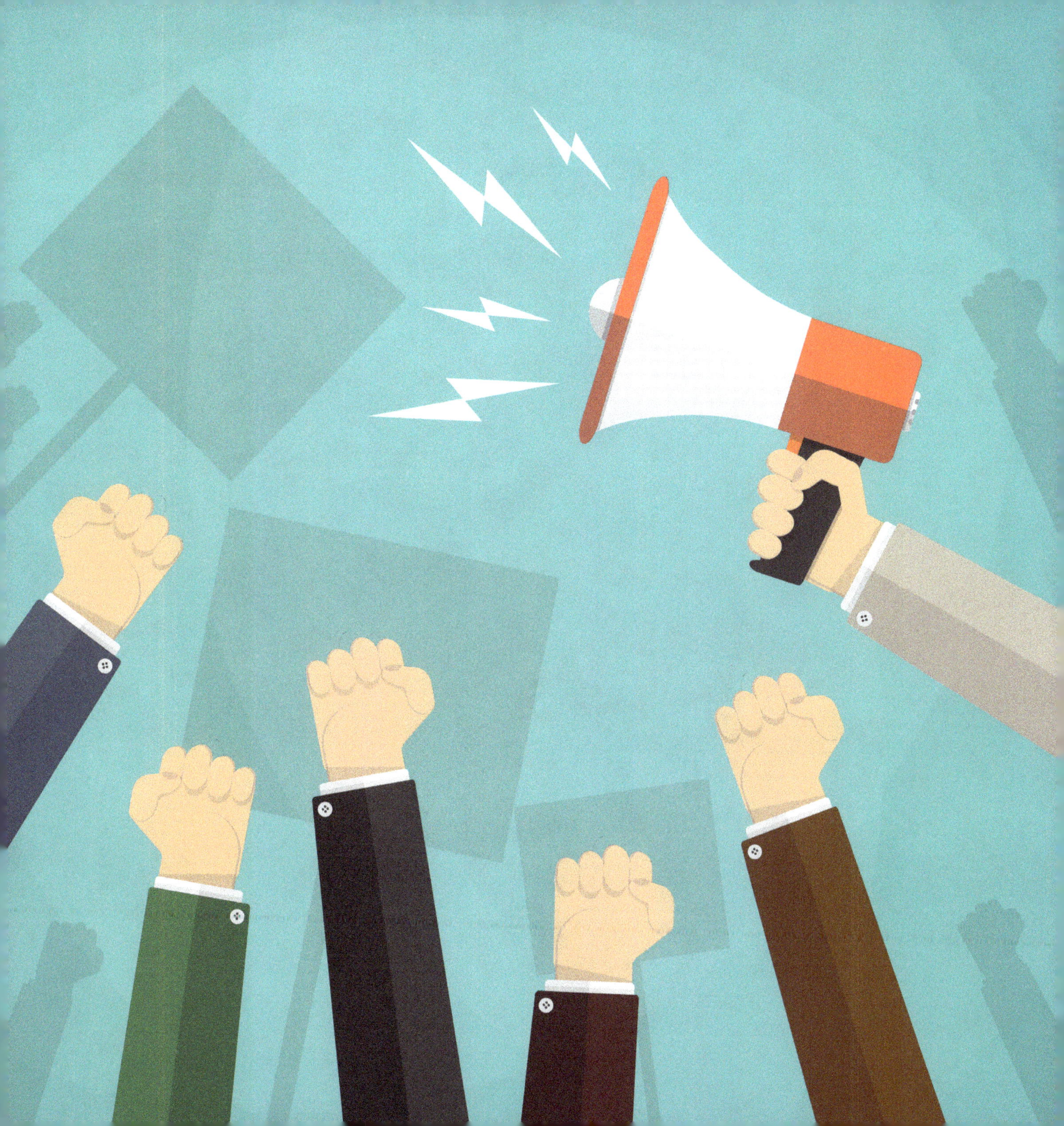

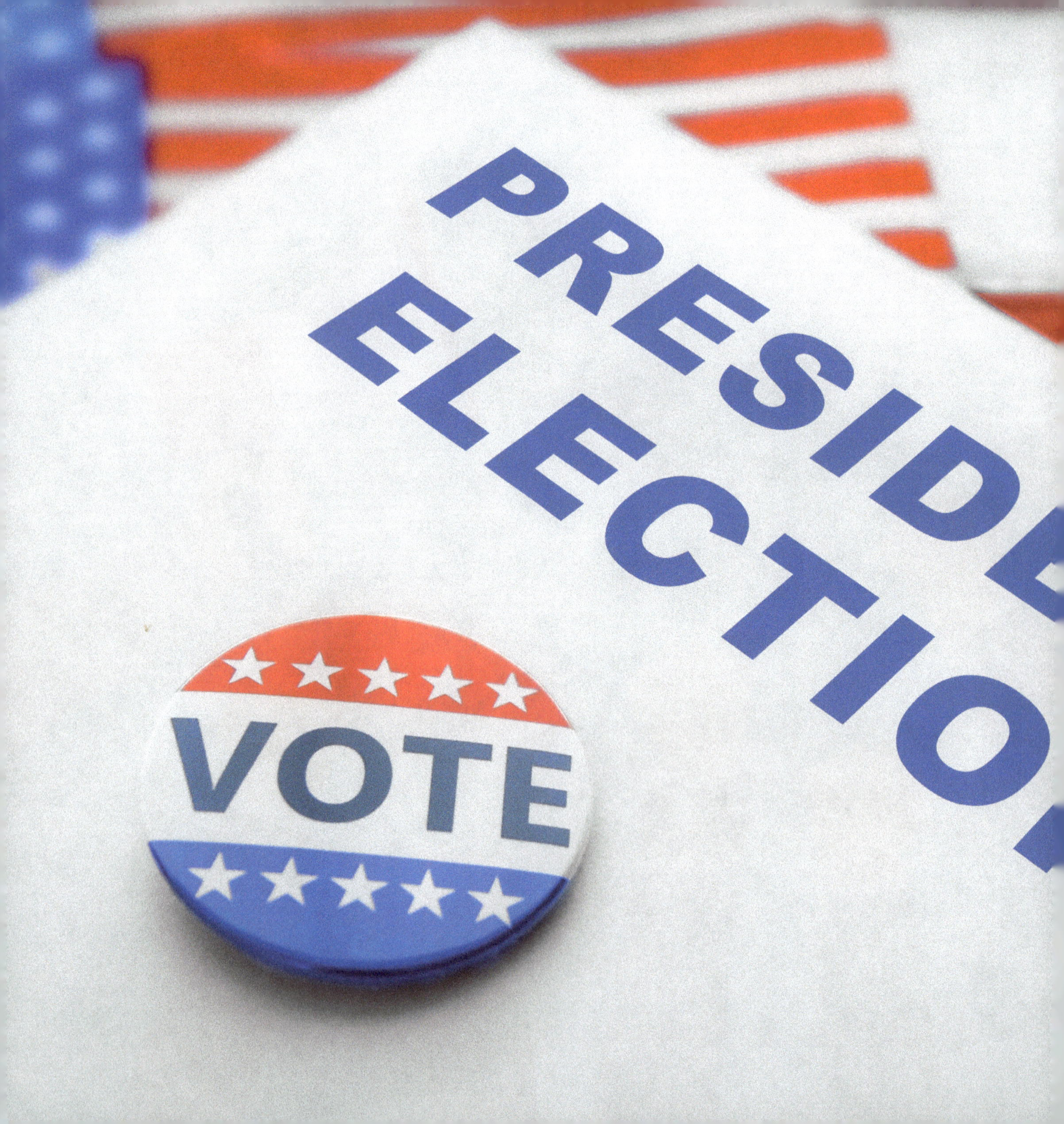
VOTE

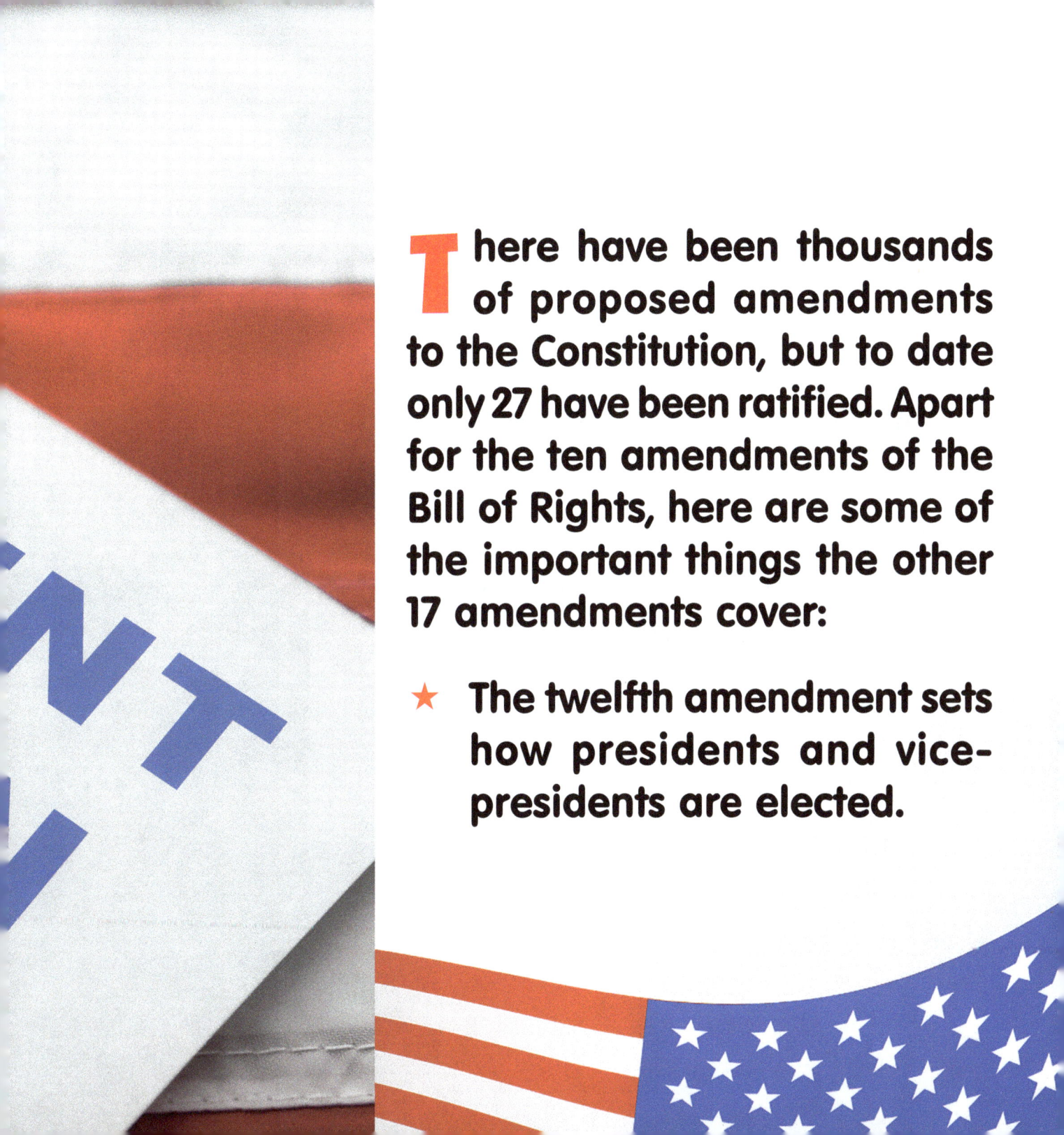

There have been thousands of proposed amendments to the Constitution, but to date only 27 have been ratified. Apart for the ten amendments of the Bill of Rights, here are some of the important things the other 17 amendments cover:

★ The twelfth amendment sets how presidents and vice-presidents are elected.

★ **The thirteenth amendment abolishes slavery in the United States. This finally happened after a bloody Civil War, eighty years after the Constitution came into effect.**

THE CIVIL WAR

FREEDMEN AT A VOTER REGISTRATION OFFICE

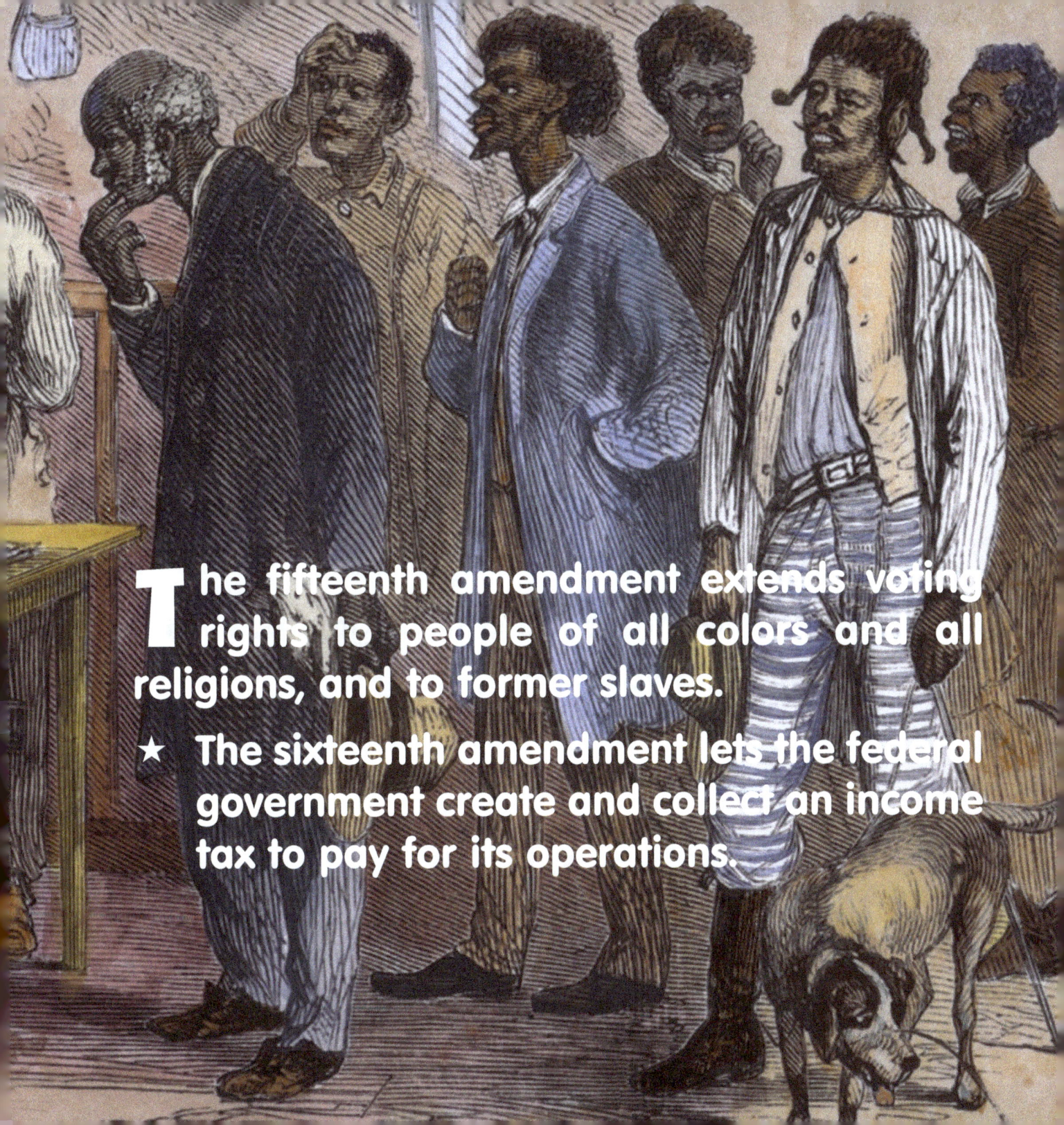

The fifteenth amendment extends voting rights to people of all colors and all religions, and to former slaves.

★ The sixteenth amendment lets the federal government create and collect an income tax to pay for its operations.

★ The eighteenth amendment prohibited selling and using alcohol—but the twenty-first amendment made it legal again!

★ The nineteenth amendment granted women the right to vote.

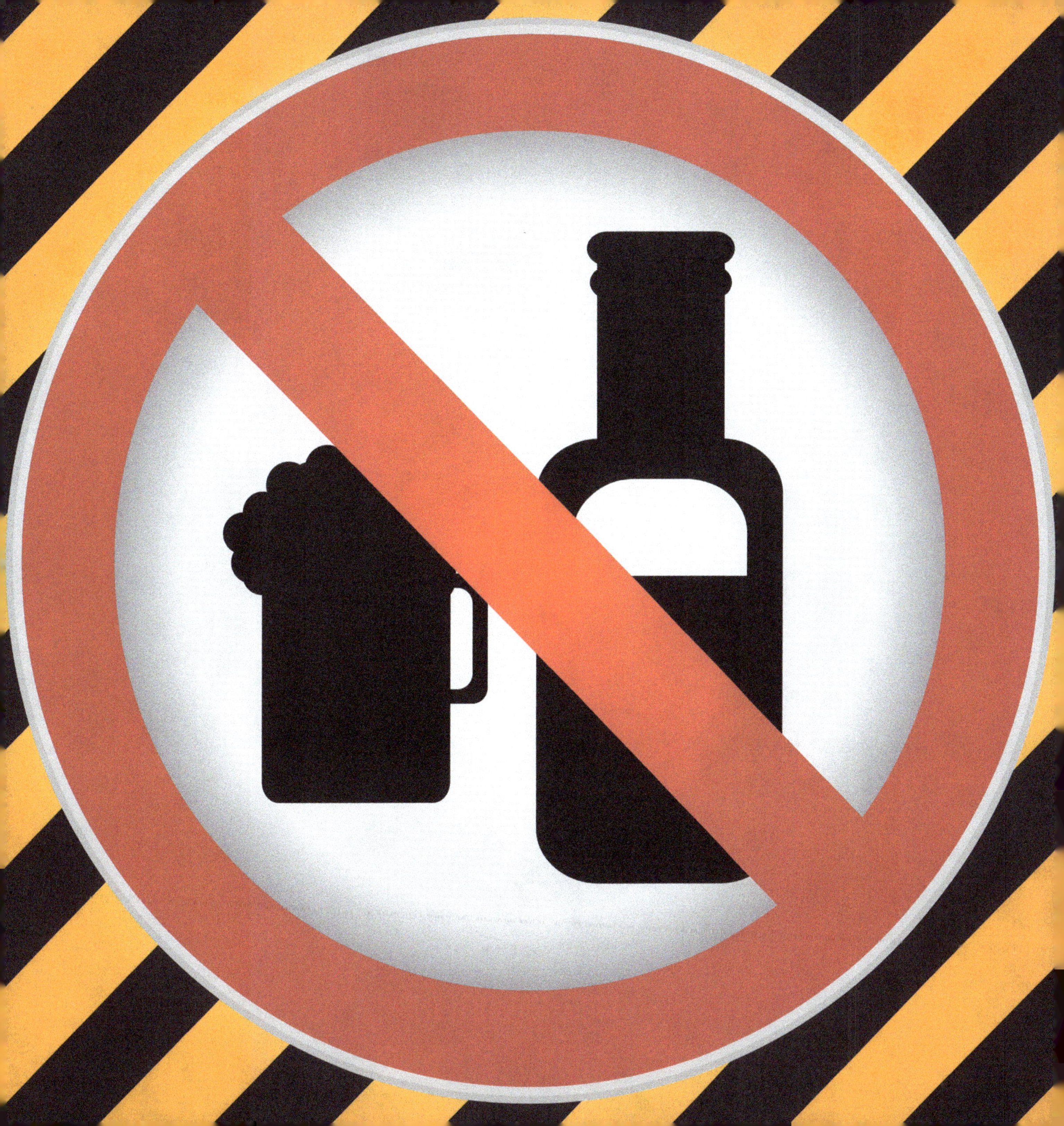

FRANKLIN ROOSEVELT

★ The twenty-second amendment states that a person can only be elected president twice. This was passed after the death of Franklin Roosevelt, who had been elected four times! Learn more about the United States Presidents in the Baby Professor book The Complete List of US Presidents from 1789 to 2016.

★ The twenty-sixth amendment lowered the voting age to eighteen.

★ The most recent amendment, the twenty-seventh, is about pay raises for members of Congress. It was proposed in 1789—and was not ratified until 1992!

Six more amendments have been approved by Congress, but have not (yet) been ratified by the states.

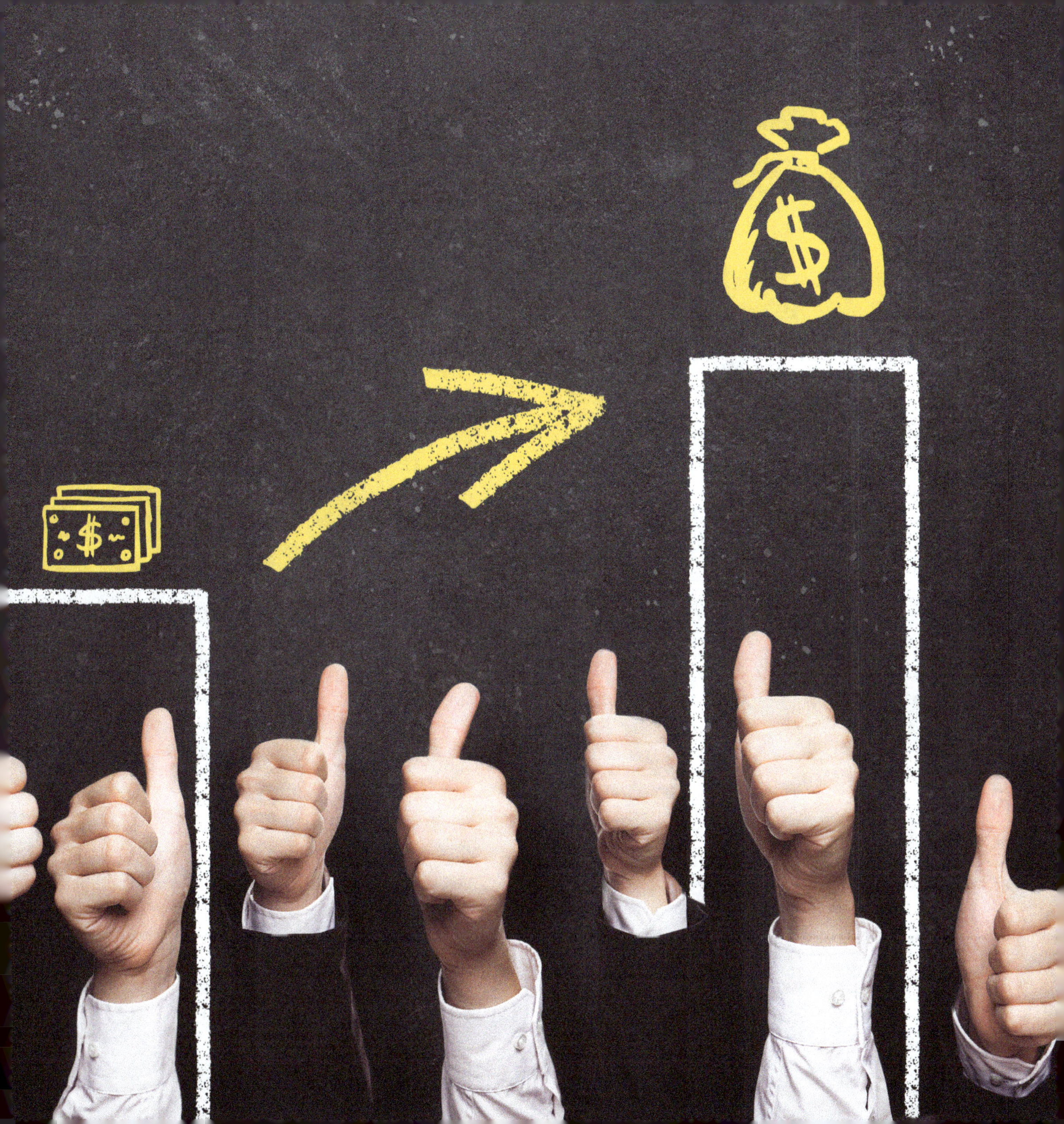

BENJAMIN FRANKLIN

CONSTITUTIONAL FACTS

★ **Eight of the delegates to the Constitutional Convention had also signed the Declaration of Independence in 1776. Six of them had signed the Articles of Confederation, which the Constitution replaced.**

★ **Benjamin Franklin, at age 81, was the oldest delegate. He was a towering figure in the early decades of the United States, as a politician, diplomat, inventor, and publisher.**

★ The youngest delegate, Jonathon Dayton of New Jersey, was twenty-six.

★ George Washington established Thanksgiving as a day for giving thanks for the creation of the Constitution.

JONATHON DAYTON

ARCHIVES OF THE UNITED STATES OF AMERICA

ARCHIVES OF THE UNITED STATES BUILDING IN WASHINGTON DC

★ The United States Constitution is the oldest written constitution establishing the government of any nation. It is also the shortest.

★ You can actually visit the original Constitution! The written document is on display at the National Archives in Washington, D.C. During times of war, it is moved to a secure location. However, if it were destroyed by a fire or some other disaster, that would not make the Constitution invalid: it is not limited to being a piece of paper!

★ George Washington, who was the president of the Constitutional Convention, almost didn't attend. He agreed that the country needed a strong central government, but he was unwell and also was not convinced that a convention could produce a good document.

GEORGE WASHINGTON

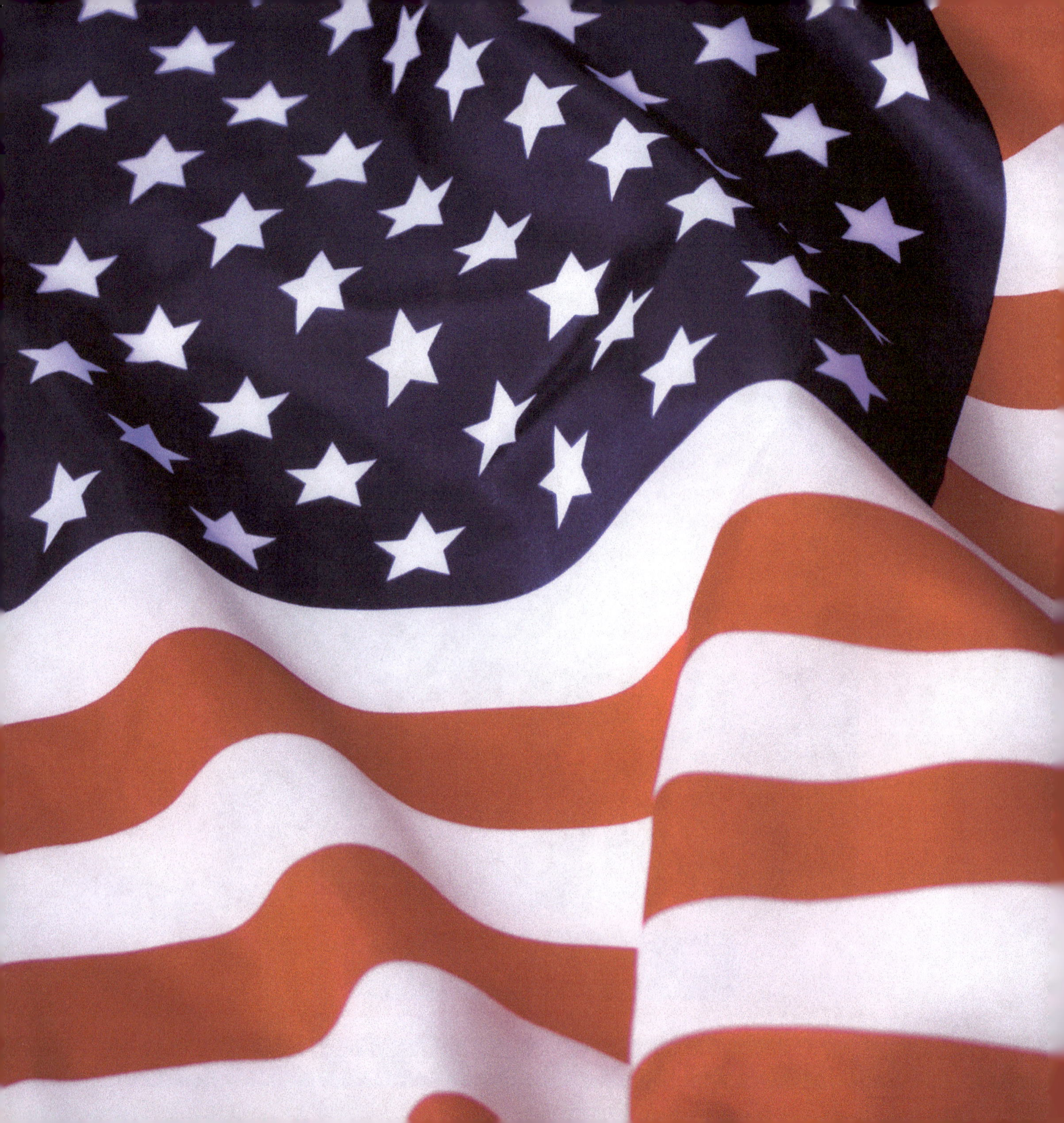

AN INSPIRING DOCUMENT

It is but truly amazing to note that the United States Constitution, a powerful document, sets how its government should work, denotes what powers each individual states possess and what legal rights every individual has.

Many other countries have been inspired by the example of the United States Constitution, and its balance of power between the executive, the legislature, and the courts.

There's another country that fought for similar freedom. Find out by reading another Baby Professor book, "The French Revolution: People Power in Action".

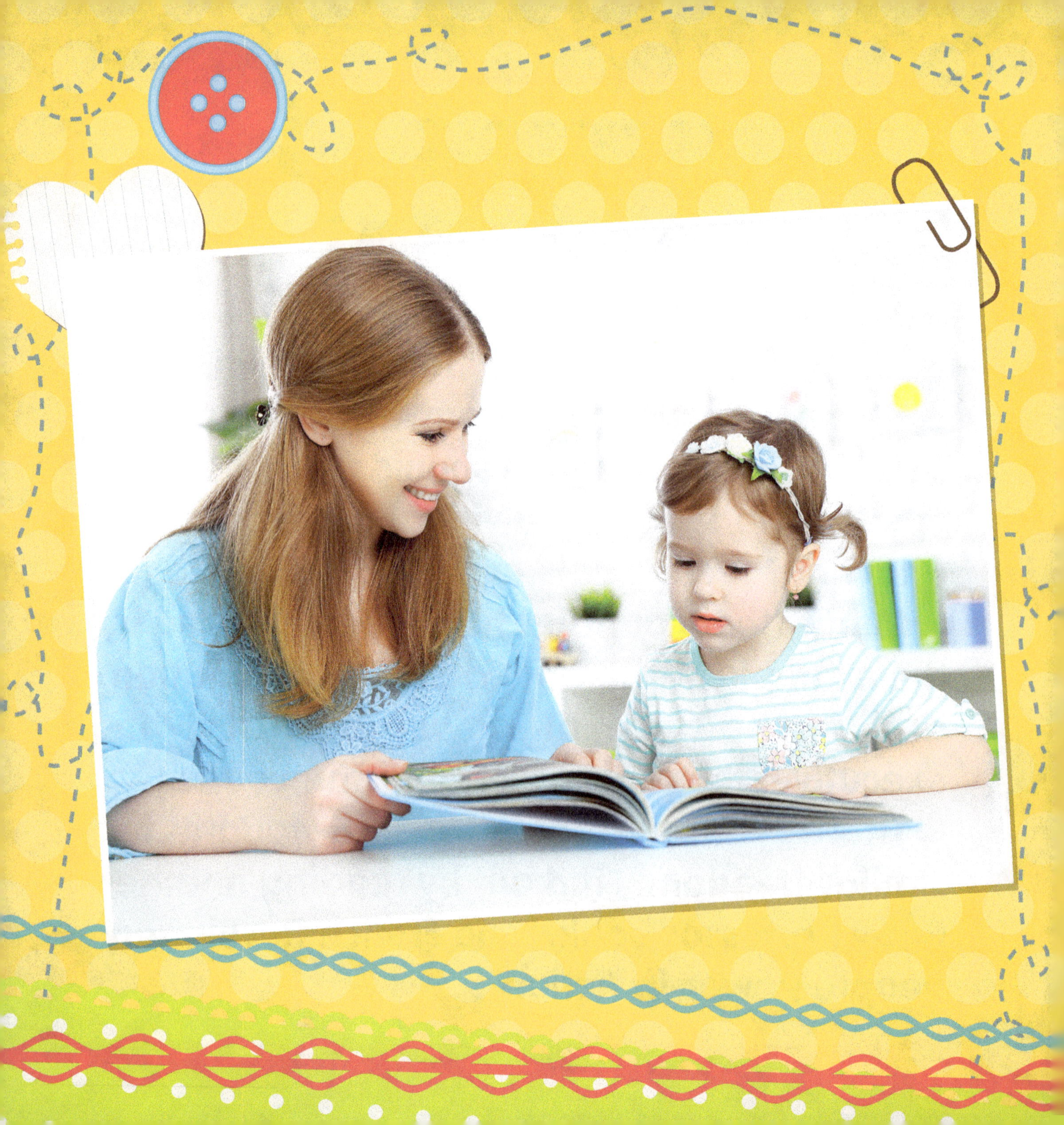

Visit

BABY PROFESSOR
EDUCATION KIDS

www.BabyProfessorBooks.com

to download Free Baby Professor eBooks and view our catalog of new and exciting Children's Books